ISBN 0-88797-521-6

Contents

Theme for Variations
(A Folk Tune)

Oleksandr O. Levytsky

Toccatina

Allegretto ♩ = 84–92

Oleksandr O. Levytsky

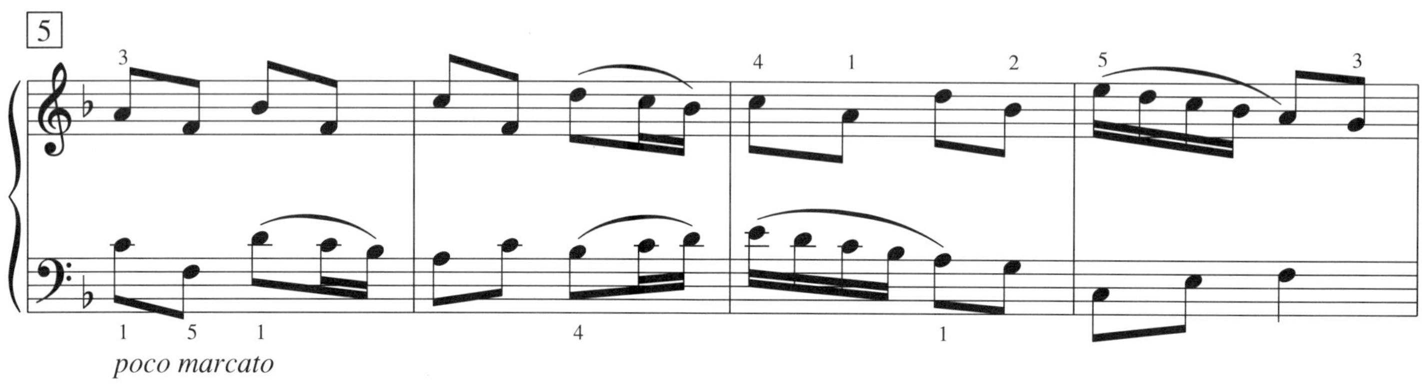

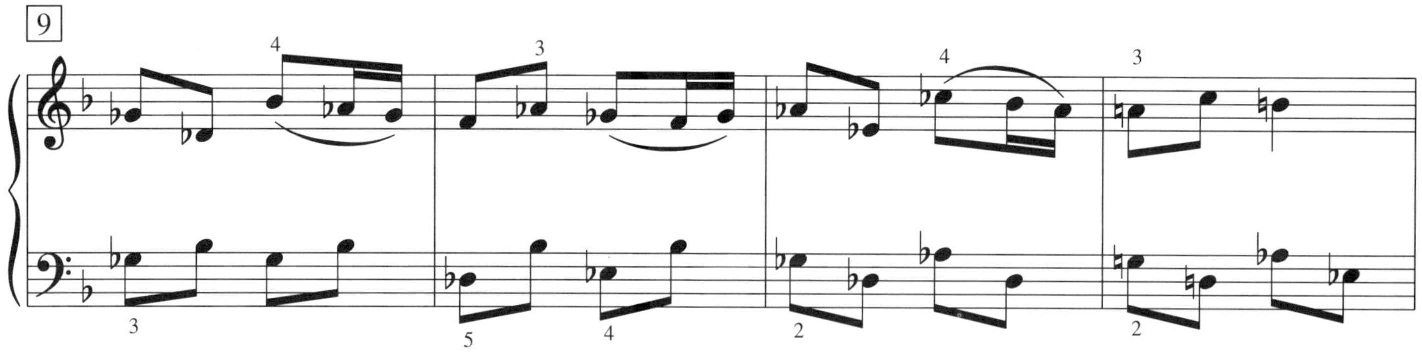

Note: Eighths without slurs are to be played detached throughout.

17
21
p
cresc.
25
f
29
f
mf
(L.H. over)
mp
p
33
cresc.
f
ff

The Merry-Go-Round

Oleksandr O. Levytsky

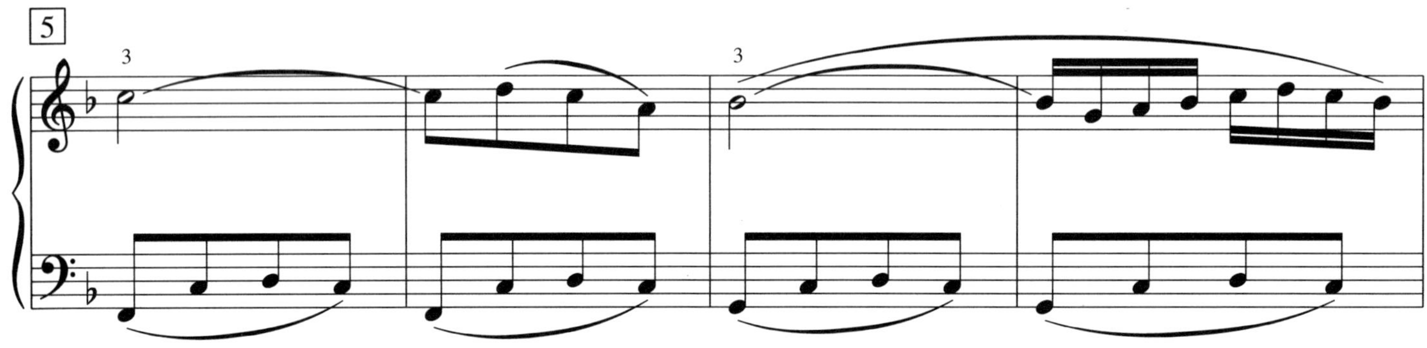

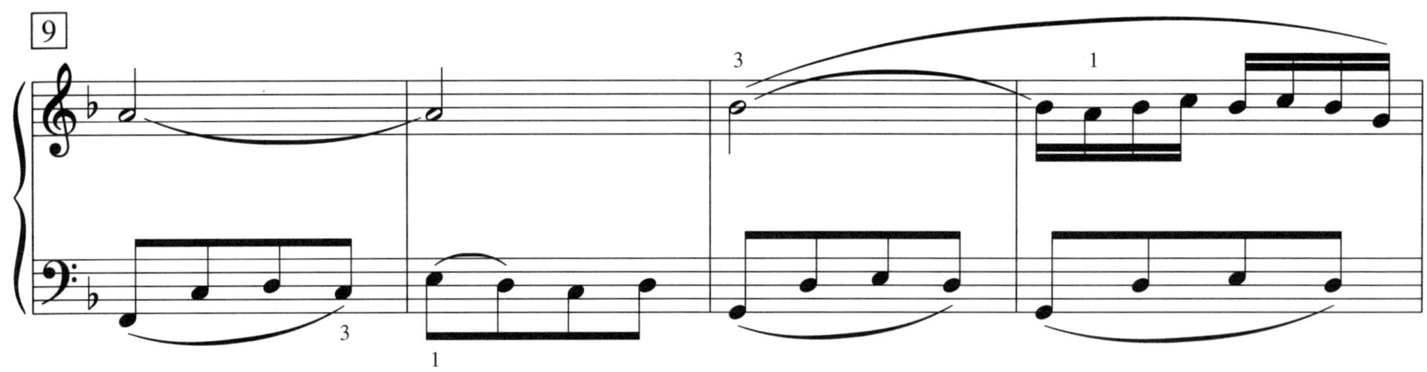

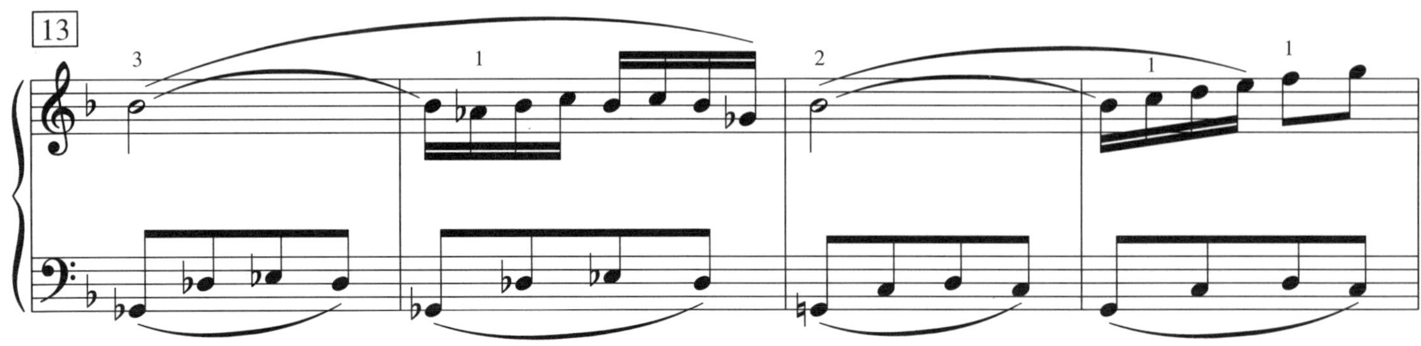

Poco più mosso ♩ = 108
17
mf
21
25
f
29
32
rit.

Tempo I
35
mf
39
43
47
2
1
1
1
3
51
5
rit.
f

A Joke

Janna Kolodub

Playing Ball

Allegretto scherzando ♩ = 104–112

Bohdana Filtz

8va
11
mf
leggiero
f
8va
16
p leggiero
rit.
21
f
26
leggiero
31
8va

A Song about Grandmother

Andante cantabile 𝅗𝅥. = 46

Bohdana Filtz

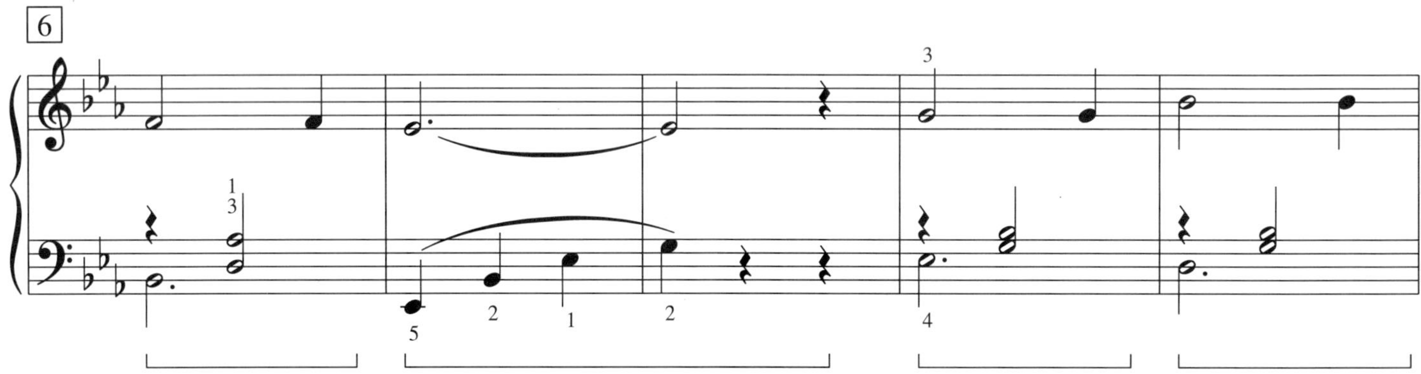

23
29
mp
34
39
44
rit.
pp
(L.H. over)

The Children's Railroad

Moderato ♩ = 126

Bohdana Filtz

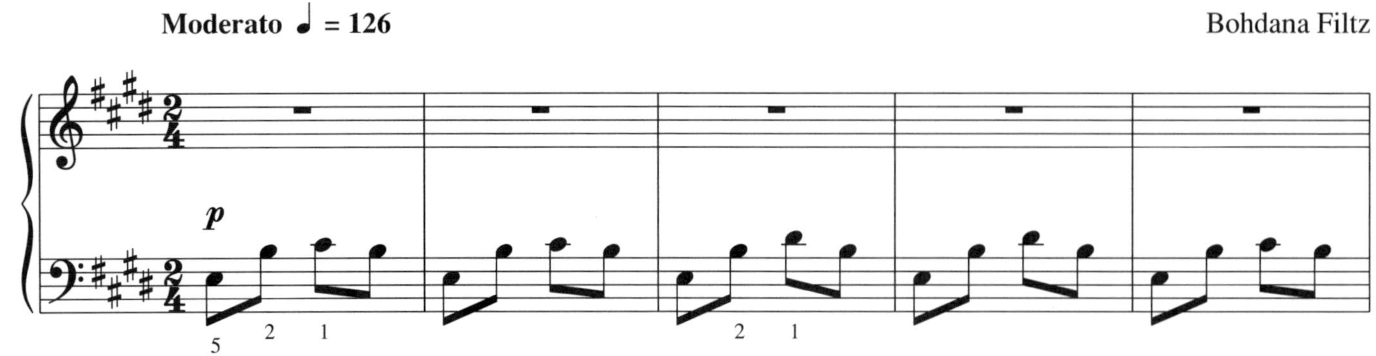

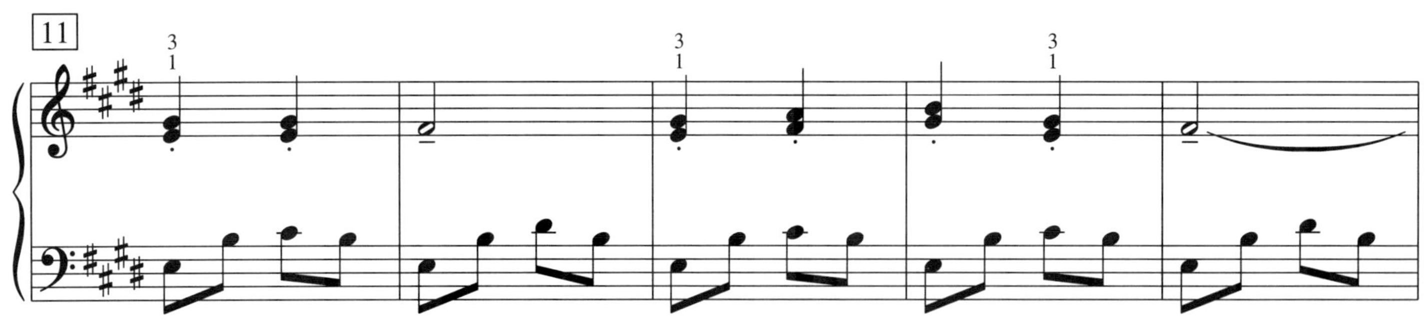

21
26
31
36
8va
41
f
mf
f

45
mf
50
p
55
f
60
p
65

71
4
3
1
1
f
77
3
mp
82
88
f
93
poco dim. e rallentando
p
99
pp

A Musical Picture

Janna Kolodub

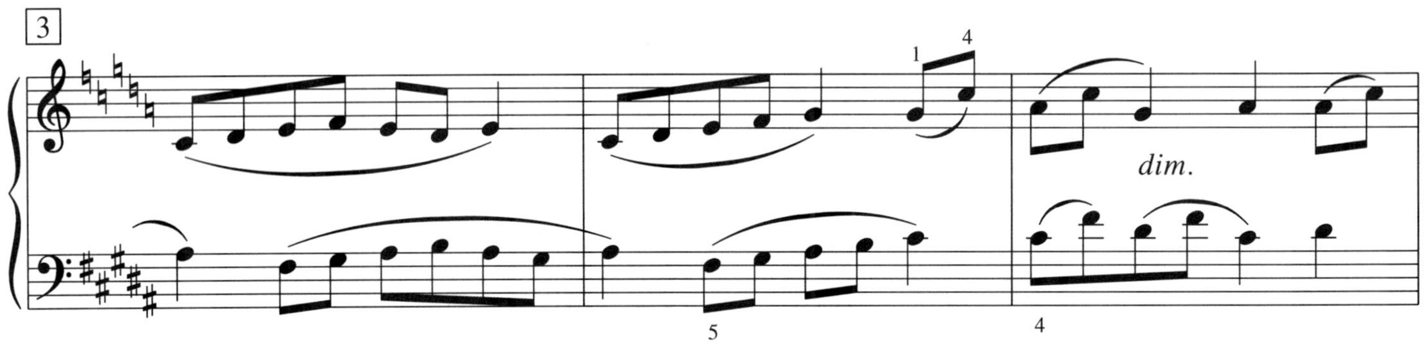

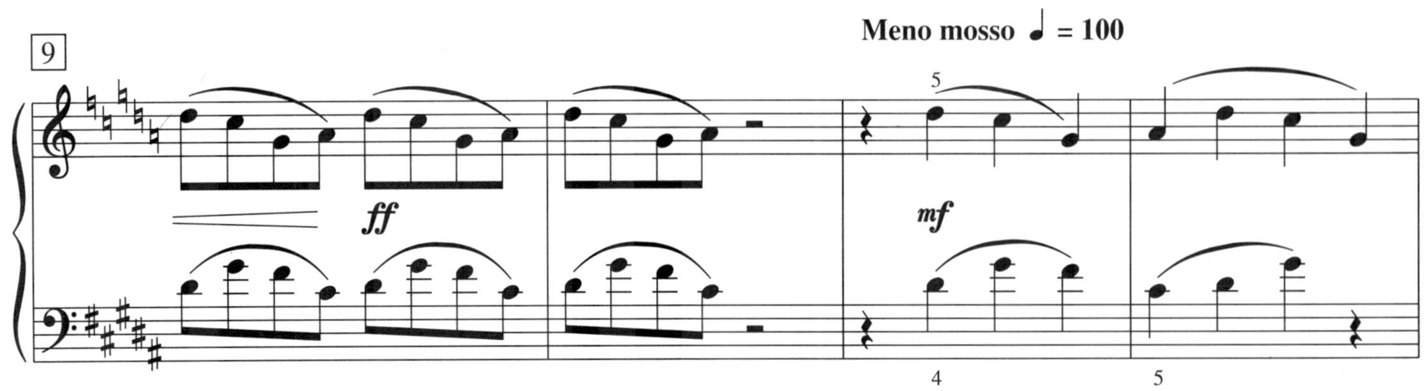

13
mp
cresc.
16
19
f
Tempo primo ♩ = 116
1
p
cresc.
4
8va bassa
23
accel.
1
2
26
f
rf

Childhood Memories

Oleksandr Levytsky's contribution to this album includes three characteristic pieces. **Theme for Variations** draws on the Ukrainian folk melody heritage, and **Toccatina** is a witty interpretation of a familiar keyboard genre, while **The Merry-Go-Round** builds a musical picture of a much-loved childhood experience. Technical challenges in **Toccatina** include bringing out the imitative entries and navigating around some tricky accidentals. Be on the lookout for subtle changes in the ostinato left-hand pattern in **The Merry-Go-Round.**

A Joke and **A Musical Picture** reveal humour in the writing of Janna Kolodub. In **A Joke,** we may be fooled into thinking the piece is over at the resounding climax in measures 17-18, but this is followed by a quiet bridge passage and a return of the opening eight measures, which provides a pleasantly rounded form. True independence of the hands is a necessity in the bi-tonal **Musical Picture.**

Bohdana Filtz's three pieces sum up the essence of happy childhood memories: a carefree afternoon's play out-of-doors, the warmth and security of a beloved grandmother's presence, and the discovery of exciting new sights and sounds. **Playing Ball** is fun; let each note ring, and think of a bouncing ball as you play the staccato notes. In contrast, **A Song about Grandmother** is in a nostalgic waltz style. Like Levytsky's piece about the merry-go-round, **The Children's Railroad** is built on an ostinato bass. You will have no doubt where the train is tooting its horn!